Contadina®

ITALIAN COOKING
QUICK · EASY · DELICIOUS

PUBLICATIONS INTERNATIONAL, LTD.

CONTADINA and LIBBY'S are registered trademarks of Nestlé U.S.A.

Favorite All Time Recipes is a trademark of Publications International, Ltd.

This edition published by Publications International, Ltd., 7373 N. Cicero Ave., Lincolnwood, IL 60646.

Photography: Sacco Productions Limited, Chicago
Photographer: Tom O'Connell
Photo Stylist: Melissa J. Frisco
Production: Paula M. Walters
Food Stylists: Amy Andrews, Carol Parik, Teri Rys-Maki
Assistant Food Stylist: Laura Hess

Pictured on the front cover: Penne with Creamy Tomato Sauce *(page 56).*

Pictured on the back cover *(top to bottom):* Lasagne Roll-Up *(page 58),* Three-Pepper Pizza *(page 8)* and Cioppino *(page 32).*

ISBN: 0-7853-1767-8

Manufactured in U.S.A.

8 7 6 5 4 3 2 1

Questions or Comments?
Please write to our
Office of Consumer Affairs
P.O. Box 29055
Glendale, CA 91209-9055

CONTENTS

WELCOME TO THE BIRTHPLACE OF FRESH IDEAS

Situated amidst the splendor of the hills of Tuscany, Italy, is Casa Buitoni, Contadina's renowned Culinary Arts Center. Here the expert chefs of Contadina, adhering to genuine traditions of Italian cuisine, create quick, easy and delicious recipes and proudly deliver them from our house to yours.

Contadina products uphold the highest standards of quality and taste — attributes that have earned Contadina a place of honor in American kitchens for generations. All of the Contadina recipes featured in this publication are examples of authentic Italian recipes that are both quick and simple — an approach to cooking preferred by today's busy cooks. Each is truly a rewarding experience, especially for those who share a love of Italian food.

When it comes to finding the freshest ideas in Italian cooking, come to Contadina.

The Freshest Ideas in Italian Cooking™

APPETIZERS & SNACKS

Authentic Italian dining starts with any one of these appetizers or pizzas featuring the traditional flavors of Italy—Italian Tomato Bread, Mozzarella and Vegetable Marinara, Three-Pepper Pizza and more. No matter what your choice, you won't be disappointed!

Three-Pepper Pizza

Makes 8 servings

1 cup (*half* of 14.5-ounce can) **CONTADINA Chunky Pizza Sauce with Three Cheeses**
1 (12-inch) pizza crust
1½ cups (6 ounces) shredded mozzarella cheese, *divided*
½ *each:* red, green and yellow bell peppers, sliced into thin rings
2 tablespoons shredded Parmesan cheese
1 tablespoon chopped fresh basil or 1 teaspoon dried basil leaves, crushed

Spread pizza sauce onto crust to within 1 inch of edge. Sprinkle with *1 cup* mozzarella cheese, bell peppers, *remaining* mozzarella cheese and Parmesan cheese. Bake according to pizza crust package directions or until crust is crisp and cheese is melted. Sprinkle with basil.

Muffin Pizza Italiano

Makes 2 servings

1 sandwich-size English muffin, split, toasted
2 tablespoons CONTADINA Pizza Squeeze
8 slices pepperoni
¼ cup sliced fresh mushrooms
¼ cup (1 ounce) shredded mozzarella cheese

Spread muffin halves with pizza squeeze. Top with pepperoni, mushrooms and cheese. Bake in preheated 400°F. oven for 8 to 10 minutes or until cheese is melted.

Three-Pepper Pizza

Pizzette with Basil

Makes about 30 pizzettes

**⅔ cup (6-ounce can)
   CONTADINA Italian-Style
   Tomato Paste
2 tablespoons (1 ounce) softened
   cream cheese
2 tablespoons chopped fresh basil
   or 2 teaspoons dried basil
   leaves, crushed
1 loaf (1 pound) Italian bread,
   sliced ¼ inch thick, toasted
8 ounces mozzarella cheese,
   thinly sliced
   Whole basil leaves (optional)
   Freshly ground black pepper
   (optional)**

In small bowl, combine tomato paste, cream cheese and chopped basil. Spread *2 teaspoons* tomato mixture onto each toasted bread slice; top with 1 slice (about ¼ ounce) mozzarella cheese. Broil 6 to 8 inches from heat for 1 to 2 minutes or until cheese begins to melt. Top with whole basil leaves and pepper, if desired.

Pizza-Stuffed Mushrooms

*Makes 12 large or 24 medium
appetizers*

**12 large or 24 medium fresh
   mushrooms
¼ cup chopped green bell pepper
¼ cup chopped pepperoni or
   cooked, crumbled Italian
   sausage
1 cup (*half* of 15-ounce can)
   CONTADINA Pizza Sauce
½ cup (2 ounces) shredded
   mozzarella cheese**

Wash and dry mushrooms; remove stems. Chop ¼ cup stems. In small bowl, combine chopped stems, bell pepper, meat and pizza sauce. Spoon mixture into mushroom caps; top with cheese. Broil 6 to 8 inches from heat for 2 to 3 minutes or until cheese is melted and mushrooms are heated through.

Pizzette with Basil

Tomato Snack Bread

Makes 6 servings

3 sandwich-size English muffins, split, toasted
1¾ cups (14.5-ounce can) CONTADINA Pasta Ready Chunky Tomatoes with Olive Oil, Garlic and Spices, undrained, *divided*
1 cup (4 ounces) shredded mozzarella cheese, *divided*

Place muffin halves on ungreased baking sheet. Spoon about *¼ cup* tomatoes and juice onto each muffin half; sprinkle with cheese. Bake in preheated 350°F. oven for 4 to 6 minutes or until cheese is melted.

Chicken and Mushroom Pizza

Makes 8 servings

1 cup (*half* of 14.5-ounce can) CONTADINA Original Chunky Pizza Sauce
1 (12-inch) pizza crust
½ teaspoon dried minced garlic
1 cup (4 ounces) shredded mozzarella cheese
4 ounces cooked chicken, chopped (about 1 cup)
1 cup sliced fresh mushrooms
½ cup (2 ounces) shredded cheddar cheese
1 tablespoon chopped fresh basil or 1 teaspoon dried basil leaves, crushed

Spread pizza sauce onto crust to within 1 inch of edge. Sprinkle with garlic, mozzarella cheese, chicken, mushrooms and cheddar cheese. Bake according to pizza crust package directions or until crust is crisp and cheese is melted. Sprinkle with basil.

Tomato Snack Bread

Tortellini Kabobs

Makes 12 servings

2 tablespoons olive or vegetable oil
1 large clove garlic, minced
2 cups (15-ounce can) CONTADINA Tomato Sauce
2 tablespoons capers
2 tablespoons chopped fresh basil or 2 teaspoons dried basil leaves, crushed
1 teaspoon Italian herb seasoning
¼ teaspoon crushed red pepper flakes
6 cups of the following kabob ingredients: cooked, drained meat- or cheese-filled tortellini, cocktail franks, smoked sausage pieces, cooked medium shrimp, whole button mushrooms, green bell pepper chunks, cooked broccoli flowerets, cauliflowerets and onion pieces

In medium skillet, heat oil. Add garlic; sauté for 30 seconds. Stir in tomato sauce, capers, basil, Italian seasoning and red pepper flakes. Bring to a boil. Reduce heat to low; simmer, uncovered, for 5 to 10 minutes or until heated through, stirring occasionally. Remove from heat. In medium bowl, combine kabob ingredients; cover with tomato sauce mixture. Cover and marinate in refrigerator for 15 minutes or longer, if desired. Remove kabob ingredients from marinade, reserving marinade. Place kabob ingredients on skewers. Broil 5 inches from heat until heated through, turning once during cooking and brushing with reserved marinade.

Mini Nacho Pizza

Makes 2 servings

1 sandwich-size English muffin, split, toasted
½ cup refried beans, *divided*
2 tablespoons CONTADINA Pizza Squeeze, *divided*
½ cup (2 ounces) shredded cheddar cheese, *divided*
2 tablespoons diced green chiles, drained (optional)

Spread each muffin half with *¼ cup* refried beans and *1 tablespoon* pizza squeeze; sprinkle with *¼ cup* cheese. Bake in preheated 400°F. oven for 10 minutes or until cheese is melted. Sprinkle with chiles, if desired.

Tortellini Kabobs

Mozzarella and Vegetable Marinara

Makes 12 servings

MOZZARELLA AND VEGETABLES
3 eggs
1¾ cups CONTADINA Seasoned Bread Crumbs
1 pound mozzarella cheese, cut into ¼-inch strips
1 medium zucchini, cut into ¼-inch strips (about 1 cup)
1 medium red or green bell pepper, cut into ¼-inch strips (about 1 cup)
Olive or vegetable oil

MARINARA SAUCE
1 tablespoon olive or vegetable oil
½ cup chopped onion
1 clove garlic, minced
2 cups (15-ounce can) CONTADINA Tomato Sauce
1 tablespoon chopped fresh basil or 1 teaspoon dried basil leaves, crushed
⅛ teaspoon crushed red pepper flakes

For Mozzarella and Vegetables: In shallow dish, beat eggs. In separate shallow dish, place bread crumbs. Dip cheese and vegetables into eggs; coat with bread crumbs. Repeat dipping into eggs and crumbs to coat again. Add enough oil to medium skillet to cover bottom to 1-inch depth. Heat oil. Add coated cheese and vegetables, a few pieces at a time, to hot oil; cook until golden brown. Remove from oil with slotted spoon. Drain on paper towels. Repeat with remaining cheese and vegetables. Serve with Marinara Sauce.

For Marinara Sauce: In small saucepan, heat oil. Add onion and garlic; sauté for 1 minute. Stir in tomato sauce, basil and red pepper flakes. Bring to a boil. Reduce heat to low; simmer, uncovered, for 10 minutes, stirring occasionally. Serve warm.

Italian Sausage and Bell Pepper Pizza

Makes 8 servings

1 cup (*half* of 14.5-ounce can) CONTADINA Chunky Pizza Sauce with Mushrooms
1 (12-inch) pizza crust
1 cup (4 ounces) shredded mozzarella cheese, *divided*
½ cup (2 ounces) shredded Parmesan cheese
4 ounces (about 2 links) mild Italian sausage, cooked and sliced or crumbled
1 small green bell pepper, cut into thin strips

Spread pizza sauce onto crust to within 1 inch of edge. Sprinkle with *½ cup* mozzarella cheese, Parmesan cheese, sausage, bell pepper and *remaining* mozzarella cheese. Bake according to pizza crust package directions or until crust is crisp and cheese is melted.

Super Chunky Pizza

Makes 8 servings

1 cup (*half* of 14.5-ounce can) CONTADINA Chunky Pizza Sauce with Three Cheeses
1 (12-inch) pizza crust
1 cup (4 ounces) cubed mozzarella cheese
1 cup (4 ounces) cubed provolone cheese
½ cup chopped red onion
6 to 8 ounces cooked ham, salami or turkey, cut into cubes
2 tablespoons chopped green onion

Spread pizza sauce onto crust to within 1 inch of edge. Top with mozzarella cheese, provolone cheese, red onion and ham. Bake according to pizza crust package directions or until crust is crisp and cheese is melted. Sprinkle with green onion.

Mediterranean Pita Pizza

Makes 6 servings

- 2 tablespoons olive or vegetable oil
- 2½ cups (8 ounces) diced, peeled eggplant
- 1 cup sliced zucchini
- 1 cup sliced fresh mushrooms
- ¼ cup chopped green bell pepper
- ¼ cup chopped onion
- 1 clove garlic, minced
- 1 cup (*half* of 15-ounce can) CONTADINA Pizza Sauce
- ½ cup sliced pitted ripe olives, drained
- ¼ teaspoon salt
- ⅛ teaspoon cayenne pepper
- 6 (6-inch) pita breads
- 1½ cups (6 ounces) shredded mozzarella or fontina cheese

In large skillet, heat oil. Add eggplant, zucchini, mushrooms, bell pepper, onion and garlic; sauté for 4 to 5 minutes or until vegetables are tender. Stir in pizza sauce, olives, salt and cayenne pepper; simmer for 5 minutes, stirring occasionally. Toast both sides of pita breads under broiler. Spoon *½ cup* vegetable mixture onto each pita bread; top with cheese. Broil 6 to 8 inches from heat for 2 to 3 minutes or until cheese is melted.

Quick and Easy Italian Sandwich

Makes 6 servings

- 1 tablespoon olive or vegetable oil
- ½ pound mild Italian sausage, casings removed, sliced ½ inch thick
- 1¾ cups (14.5-ounce can) CONTADINA Pasta Ready Chunky Tomatoes with Olives, undrained
- ½ cup sliced green bell pepper
- 6 sandwich-size English muffins, split, toasted
- ¼ cup (1 ounce) shredded Parmesan cheese, *divided*

In medium skillet, heat oil. Add sausage; cook for 3 to 4 minutes or until no longer pink in center, stirring occasionally. Drain. Add tomatoes and juice and bell pepper; simmer, uncovered, for 5 minutes, stirring occasionally. Spread *½ cup* meat mixture onto each of 6 muffin halves; sprinkle with Parmesan cheese. Top with remaining muffin halves.

Mediterranean Pita Pizzas

Sicilian Caponata

Makes 4½ cups

5 tablespoons olive or vegetable oil, *divided*
8 cups (1½ pounds) cubed unpeeled eggplant
2½ cups onion slices
1 cup chopped celery
1¾ cups (14.5-ounce can) CONTADINA Pasta Ready Chunky Tomatoes with Olive Oil, Garlic and Spices, undrained
⅓ cup chopped pitted ripe olives, drained
¼ cup balsamic or red wine vinegar
2 tablespoons capers
2 teaspoons granulated sugar
½ teaspoon salt
Dash of ground black pepper

In medium skillet, heat *3 tablespoons* oil. Add eggplant; sauté for 6 minutes. Remove eggplant from skillet. In same skillet, heat *remaining* oil. Add onion and celery; sauté for 5 minutes or until vegetables are tender. Stir in tomatoes and juice and eggplant; cover. Bring to a boil. Reduce heat to low; simmer for 15 minutes or until eggplant is tender. Stir in olives, vinegar, capers, sugar, salt and pepper; simmer, uncovered, for 5 minutes, stirring occasionally.

Barbecue Dipping Sauce

Makes about 2 cups

1¾ cups (15-ounce can) CONTADINA Pizza Sauce
¼ cup firmly packed brown sugar
2 tablespoons vinegar
1 tablespoon prepared mustard
½ teaspoon liquid smoke

In medium saucepan, combine pizza sauce, brown sugar, vinegar, mustard and liquid smoke. Bring to a boil. Reduce heat to low; simmer, uncovered, for 5 minutes, stirring occasionally. Serve with chicken nuggets, meatballs, shrimp or cocktail franks, if desired.

Sicilian Caponata

Classic Pepperoni Pizza

Makes 8 servings

1 cup (*half* of 14.5-ounce can) CONTADINA Chunky Pizza Sauce with Mushrooms
1 (12-inch) pizza crust
1½ cups (6 ounces) shredded mozzarella cheese, *divided*
1.5 ounces (about 25 slices) sliced pepperoni
1 tablespoon chopped fresh parsley

Spread pizza sauce onto crust to within 1 inch of edge. Sprinkle with *1 cup* cheese, pepperoni and *remaining* cheese. Bake according to pizza crust package directions or until crust is crisp and cheese is melted. Sprinkle with parsley.

Three-Way Salsa

Makes about 5 cups

3½ cups (*two* 14.5-ounce cans) CONTADINA Recipe Ready Diced Tomatoes, undrained
1 cup (8-ounce can) CONTADINA Tomato Sauce
1 large onion, finely chopped (about 1 cup)
½ cup (4-ounce can) diced green chiles, drained
⅓ cup chopped green bell pepper
1 large clove garlic, minced
2 tablespoons chopped fresh cilantro
½ teaspoon cumin
½ teaspoon salt
¼ teaspoon ground black pepper

In medium bowl, combine tomatoes and juice, tomato sauce, onion, chiles, bell pepper, garlic, cilantro, cumin, salt and black pepper; cover. Chill thoroughly. Serve with tortilla chips, cut-up fresh vegetables or bread sticks, if desired.

Note: For medium-hot salsa, add ½ to 1 teaspoon minced jalapeño peppers. For very hot salsa, add 2 to 3 teaspoons minced jalapeño peppers and 10 drops hot pepper sauce.

Classic Pepperoni Pizza

Calzone Italiano

Makes 4 servings

Pizza dough for one 14-inch pizza
1¾ **cups (15-ounce can) CONTADINA Pizza Sauce,** *divided*
3 **ounces sliced pepperoni** *or* ½ **pound crumbled Italian sausage, cooked, drained**
2 **tablespoons chopped green bell pepper**
1 **cup (4 ounces) shredded mozzarella cheese**
1 **cup (8 ounces) ricotta cheese**

Divide dough into 4 equal portions. Place on lightly floured, large, rimless cookie sheet. Press or roll out dough to 7-inch circles. Spread *2 tablespoons* pizza sauce onto half of each circle to within ½ inch of edge; top with ¼ each: pepperoni, bell pepper and mozzarella cheese. Spoon ¼ cup ricotta cheese onto remaining half of each circle; fold dough over. Press edges together tightly to seal. Cut slits into top of dough to allow steam to escape. Bake in preheated 350°F. oven for 20 to 25 minutes or until crusts are golden brown. Meanwhile, heat *remaining* pizza sauce; serve over calzones.

Note: If desired, 1 large calzone may be made instead of 4 individual calzones. To prepare, shape dough into 1 (13-inch) circle. Spread ½ *cup* pizza sauce onto half of dough; proceed as above. Bake for 25 minutes.

Chunky Three-Cheese and Chicken Pizza

Makes 8 servings

1 **cup (***half* **of 14.5-ounce can) CONTADINA Chunky Original Pizza Sauce**
1 **(12-inch) pizza crust**
4 **ounces cooked chicken, chopped (about 1 cup)**
1 **cup (4 ounces) cubed mozzarella cheese**
½ **cup (2 ounces) cubed cheddar cheese**
¼ **cup (1 ounce) shredded Parmesan cheese**
2 **tablespoons chopped fresh basil** **or 2 teaspoons dried basil leaves, crushed (optional)**

Spread pizza sauce onto crust to within 1 inch of edge. Top with chicken, mozzarella cheese, cheddar cheese and Parmesan cheese. Bake according to pizza crust package directions or until crust is crisp and cheese is melted. Sprinkle with basil, if desired.

Calzone Italiano

Stuffed Pizza Pie

Makes 8 servings

Pastry for double crust 10-inch pie

5 **eggs, lightly beaten**

2 **cups (15-ounce container) ricotta cheese**

1 **cup (4 ounces) grated Parmesan cheese**

¼ **cup chopped onion**

2 **tablespoons chopped fresh parsley or 2 teaspoons dried parsley flakes**

1 **large clove garlic, minced**

1¾ **cups (15-ounce can) CONTADINA Pizza Sauce**

1 **teaspoon Italian herb seasoning**

½ **pound thinly sliced mozzarella cheese, *divided***

½ **cup sliced pitted ripe olives, drained**

1 **small green bell pepper, cut into strips**

Prepare pastry; divide in half. On lightly floured surface, roll out *half* of pastry to 12-inch circle; place on bottom and up side of 10-inch deep-dish pie plate. Roll out *remaining* pastry to 12-inch circle; cover and set aside. In medium bowl, combine eggs, ricotta cheese, Parmesan cheese, onion, parsley and garlic. In small bowl, combine pizza sauce and Italian seasoning. Spread *half* of ricotta cheese mixture onto bottom of pie shell; cover with layers of *half* of the sauce, mozzarella cheese, olives and bell pepper strips. Repeat layers. Top with remaining pie crust; flute edges. Cut slits into top crust to allow steam to escape. Bake in preheated 425°F. oven for 40 to 45 minutes or until crust is lightly browned. Let stand for 20 minutes before cutting into slices to serve.

Italian Tomato Bread

Makes about 24 appetizers

3½ cups (*two* 14.5-ounce cans)
   CONTADINA Pasta Ready
   Chunky Tomatoes with Three
   Cheeses, drained
¼ cup sliced green onions
1 loaf (1 pound) Italian or French
   bread
1½ cups (6 ounces) shredded
   mozzarella cheese

In medium bowl, combine tomatoes and green onions. Cut bread in half lengthwise. Scoop out ½-inch layer of bread to within 1 inch of side crusts; reserve removed bread for another use. Spoon tomato mixture equally into bread shells; top with cheese. Place on ungreased baking sheet. Bake in preheated 450°F. oven for 5 to 8 minutes or until heated through and cheese is melted. Cut diagonally into 1-inch-thick slices.

Chunky Primavera Pizza

Makes 8 servings

1 cup (*half* of 14.5-ounce can)
   CONTADINA Chunky Pizza
   Sauce with Mushrooms
1 (12-inch) pizza crust
½ teaspoon dried thyme leaves,
   crushed
1½ cups (6 ounces) shredded
   mozzarella cheese, *divided*
2 to 3 cups fresh vegetables (red,
   yellow or green bell pepper
   chunks, cut cooked
   asparagus, broccoli or
   cauliflower chunks)
2 tablespoons chopped green
   onion
¼ cup roasted cashews, halved

Spread pizza sauce onto crust to within 1 inch of edge. Sprinkle with thyme, *1 cup* cheese, vegetables, green onion, cashews and *remaining* cheese. Bake according to pizza crust package directions or until crust is crisp and cheese is melted.

SOUPS & SALADS

In search of a quick-to-fix meal that is light, yet satisfying? Nothing hits the spot better than a thick, robust minestrone, a beautifully arranged antipasto salad or a fresh-from-the-sea cioppino. Page through this first-rate collection of savory soups and satisfying main-dish salads for creative recipe ideas.

Minestrone

Makes 8 cups

3 slices bacon, diced
½ cup chopped onion
1 large clove garlic, minced
2½ cups (*two* 10½-ounce cans) beef broth
1½ cups water
1¾ cups (15½-ounce can) Great Northern white beans, undrained
⅔ cup (6-ounce can) CONTADINA Tomato Paste
1 teaspoon Italian herb seasoning
¼ teaspoon ground black pepper
2 medium zucchini, sliced (about 2 cups)
1 package (10 ounces) frozen mixed vegetables
½ cup elbow macaroni, uncooked
½ cup (2 ounces) grated Parmesan cheese (optional)

In large saucepan, sauté bacon until crisp. Add onion and garlic; sauté until onion is tender. Add broth, water, beans and liquid, tomato paste, Italian seasoning and pepper. Reduce heat to low; simmer, uncovered, for 10 minutes. Add zucchini, mixed vegetables and macaroni. Return to a boil over high heat, stirring to break up vegetables. Reduce heat to low; simmer for 8 to 10 minutes or until vegetables and macaroni are tender. Sprinkle with Parmesan cheese just before serving, if desired.

Minestrone

Sicilian-Style Pasta Salad

Makes 10 servings

1 pound dry rotini pasta, cooked, drained, chilled

3½ cups (*two* 14.5-ounce cans) CONTADINA Pasta Ready Chunky Tomatoes with Crushed Red Pepper or Pasta Ready Chunky Tomatoes with Three Cheeses, undrained

1 cup sliced yellow bell pepper

1 cup halved zucchini slices

8 ounces cooked bay shrimp

½ cup (2.25-ounce can) sliced pitted ripe olives, drained

2 tablespoons balsamic vinegar

In large bowl, combine pasta, tomatoes and juice, bell pepper, zucchini, shrimp, olives and vinegar; toss well. Cover. Chill before serving.

Easy Antipasto Salad

Makes 6 servings

1¾ cups (14.5-ounce can) CONTADINA Stewed Tomatoes, drained

½ cup thinly sliced cucumber

½ cup thinly sliced onion

1 cup (*two* 6-ounce jars) marinated artichoke hearts, drained, cut in half

1 ounce thinly sliced salami (optional)

½ cup sliced pitted ripe olives, drained

½ cup thinly sliced green bell pepper

½ cup Italian dressing

In 1-quart casserole dish, layer tomatoes, cucumber, onion, artichoke hearts, salami, olives and bell pepper. Pour dressing over salad; cover. Chill before serving.

Southern Italian Clam Chowder

Makes 8 cups

2 slices bacon, diced

1 cup chopped onion

½ cup chopped peeled carrots

½ cup chopped celery

3½ cups (*two* 14.5-ounce cans) CONTADINA Recipe Ready Diced Tomatoes, undrained

1 cup (8-ounce can) CONTADINA Tomato Sauce

1 cup (8-ounce bottle) clam juice

½ teaspoon chopped fresh rosemary or ¼ teaspoon dried rosemary leaves, crushed

⅛ teaspoon ground black pepper

1½ cups (*two* 6½-ounce cans) chopped clams, undrained

In large saucepan, sauté bacon until crisp. Add onion, carrots and celery; sauté for 2 to 3 minutes or until vegetables are tender. Stir in tomatoes and juice, tomato sauce, clam juice, rosemary and pepper. Bring to a boil. Reduce heat to low; simmer, uncovered, for 15 minutes. Stir in clams and juice. Simmer for 5 minutes or until heated through.

Sicilian-Style Pasta Salad

Cioppino

Makes about 14 cups

2 tablespoons olive or vegetable oil
1½ cups chopped onion
1 cup chopped celery
½ cup chopped green bell pepper
1 large clove garlic, minced
3½ cups (28-ounce can) CONTADINA Whole Peeled Tomatoes, undrained
⅔ cup (6-ounce can) CONTADINA Tomato Paste
1 teaspoon Italian herb seasoning
1 teaspoon salt
½ teaspoon ground black pepper
2 cups water
1 cup dry red wine or chicken broth
3 pounds white fish, shrimp, scallops, cooked crab, cooked lobster, clams and/or oysters (in any proportion)

In large saucepan, heat oil. Add onion, celery, bell pepper and garlic; sauté until vegetables are tender. Add tomatoes and juice, tomato paste, Italian seasoning, salt, black pepper, water and wine. Break up tomatoes with spoon. Bring to a boil. Reduce heat to low; simmer, uncovered, for 15 minutes. To prepare fish and seafood: Scrub clams and oysters under running water. Place in ½ inch boiling water in separate large saucepan; cover. Bring to a boil. Reduce heat to low; simmer just until shells open, about 3 minutes. Set aside. Cut crab, lobster, fish and scallops into bite-sized pieces. Shell and devein shrimp.

Add fish to tomato mixture; simmer for 5 minutes. Add scallops and shrimp; simmer for 5 minutes. Add crab, lobster and reserved clams; simmer until heated through.

Milan Chickpea Soup

Makes about 10 cups

⅔ cup (6-ounce can) CONTADINA Tomato Paste
4 cups water or chicken broth
3½ cups (*two* 15½-ounce cans) chickpeas or garbanzo beans, undrained
½ pound mild Italian sausage, casings removed, sliced ½ inch thick
1 cup sliced fresh mushrooms
1 cup chopped onion
1½ teaspoons salt
¼ teaspoon ground black pepper
¼ teaspoon marjoram
2 teaspoons grated Parmesan cheese

In large saucepan, combine tomato paste and water; stir until well blended. Add chickpeas and liquid, sausage, mushrooms, onion, salt, pepper and marjoram; stir. Cover. Bring to a boil. Reduce heat to low; simmer for 30 minutes, stirring occasionally. Sprinkle with Parmesan cheese just before serving.

Cioppino

Layered Chicken Salad

Makes 6 to 8 servings

3½ cups (*two* 14.5-ounce cans)
     CONTADINA Stewed
     Tomatoes, undrained
4 cups torn salad greens
2 cups sliced fresh mushrooms
4 cups cubed cooked chicken
     (about 4 boneless, skinless
     chicken breast halves)
1 cup sliced red onion
2½ cups (16-ounce package) frozen
     peas, thawed
½ cup sliced cucumber
1½ cups mayonnaise
1 teaspoon seasoned salt
¾ teaspoon dried tarragon leaves,
     crushed
⅛ teaspoon ground black pepper

Drain tomatoes, reserving 2
tablespoons juice. Layer ingredients
in large salad bowl as follows:
greens, mushrooms, drained
tomatoes, chicken, onion, peas and
cucumber. In small bowl, combine
mayonnaise, reserved juice,
seasoned salt, tarragon and pepper;
blend well. Spread mayonnaise
mixture over top of salad; cover with
plastic wrap. Chill for several hours
or overnight.

Bean and Rice Soup

Makes 10 cups

3 ounces thinly sliced pancetta,
     chopped (about ½ cup)
1 cup chopped onion
2 quarts (*four* 10½-ounce cans)
     beef broth
3½ cups (*two* 14.5-ounce cans)
     CONTADINA Pasta Ready
     Chunky Tomatoes with Olive
     Oil, Garlic and Spices,
     undrained
1 tablespoon chopped fresh
     rosemary or 1 teaspoon dried
     rosemary leaves, crushed
1 cup arborio or long-grain white
     rice, uncooked
¼ teaspoon salt
¼ teaspoon ground black pepper
1¾ cups (15½-ounce can) Great
     Northern white beans,
     drained
2 tablespoons chopped fresh
     Italian parsley

In large saucepan, sauté pancetta for
1 minute. Add onion; sauté for 2 to 3
minutes or just until pancetta is
crisp. Add broth, tomatoes and juice
and rosemary. Bring to a boil.
Reduce heat to low; simmer,
uncovered, for 10 minutes. Add rice,
salt and pepper; simmer, covered, for
20 to 25 minutes or until rice is
tender. Add beans; simmer for 5
minutes. Sprinkle with parsley just
before serving.

Note: Substitute 3 bacon slices for
3 ounces pancetta.

Layered Chicken Salad

Spicy Shrimp Cocktail

Makes 6 servings

- 2 tablespoons olive or vegetable oil
- ¼ cup finely chopped onion
- 1 tablespoon chopped green bell pepper
- 1 clove garlic, minced
- 1 cup (8-ounce can) CONTADINA Tomato Sauce
- 1 tablespoon chopped pitted green olives, drained
- ¼ teaspoon crushed red pepper flakes
- 1 pound cooked shrimp, chilled

In small skillet, heat oil. Add onion, bell pepper and garlic; sauté until vegetables are tender. Stir in tomato sauce, olives and red pepper flakes. Bring to a boil. Reduce heat to low; simmer, uncovered, for 5 minutes. Cover. Chill thoroughly. Just before serving, combine sauce with shrimp in small bowl. Serve over mixed greens, if desired.

Tomato-Lentil Soup

Makes 9 cups

- 2 tablespoons olive or vegetable oil
- 2 cups chopped onion
- 1 cup sliced celery
- 1 carrot, peeled, sliced
- 6 cups water
- 1 cup dry lentils
- ⅔ cup (6-ounce can) CONTADINA Tomato Paste
- ½ cup dry red wine or chicken broth
- ¼ cup chopped fresh parsley or 1 tablespoon dried parsley flakes
- 3 small (½ ounce total) chicken bouillon cubes
- 1 teaspoon salt
- ½ teaspoon Worcestershire sauce
- ¼ teaspoon ground black pepper Shredded or grated Parmesan cheese (optional)

In large saucepan, heat oil over medium-high heat. Add onion, celery and carrot; sauté until vegetables are tender. Stir in water, lentils, tomato paste, wine, parsley, bouillon cubes, salt, Worcestershire sauce and pepper. Bring to a boil. Reduce heat to low; simmer, uncovered, for 45 to 50 minutes or until lentils are tender. Sprinkle with Parmesan cheese, if desired.

Spicy Shrimp Cocktail

Cool Italian Tomato Soup

Makes 6 cups

1¾ cups (14.5-ounce can)
CONTADINA Pasta Ready
Chunky Tomatoes with
Crushed Red Pepper,
undrained
2 cups tomato juice
½ cup half-and-half
2 tablespoons lemon juice
1 large cucumber, peeled, diced
(about 2 cups)
1 medium green bell pepper,
diced (about ½ cup)
Chopped fresh basil (optional)
Croutons (optional)

In blender container, place tomatoes and juice, tomato juice, half-and-half and lemon juice; blend until smooth. Pour into large bowl or soup tureen; stir in cucumber and bell pepper. Sprinkle with basil and croutons just before serving, if desired.

Seafood Salad

Makes 6 servings

4 tablespoons olive or vegetable
oil, *divided*
½ cup diced onion
2 cloves garlic, minced
8 ounces medium shrimp, peeled,
deveined
8 ounces medium scallops
¼ teaspoon salt
¼ teaspoon ground black pepper
1 cup Italian bread cubes
1¾ cups (14.5-ounce can)
CONTADINA Recipe Ready
Diced Tomatoes, drained
2 cups torn salad greens
1 cup yellow bell pepper, cut into
strips
2 tablespoons chopped fresh
Italian parsley
1 tablespoon white wine vinegar

In medium skillet, heat *1 tablespoon* oil. Add onion and garlic; sauté for 1 minute. Add shrimp, scallops, salt and black pepper; sauté for 3 minutes. Remove from heat. In small skillet, heat *1 tablespoon* oil. Add bread cubes; sauté until golden brown. In large bowl, place seafood mixture, tomatoes, greens, bell pepper, parsley, *remaining* oil and vinegar; toss lightly. Top with bread cubes.

Cool Italian Tomato Soup

Chickpea and Shrimp Soup

Makes 12 cups

- 1 tablespoon olive or vegetable oil
- 1 cup diced onion
- 2 cloves garlic, minced
- 2 quarts (*four* 10½-ounce cans) beef broth
- 1¾ cups (14.5-ounce can) CONTADINA Pasta Ready Chunky Tomatoes with Olive Oil, Garlic and Spices, undrained
- 1¾ cups (15½-ounce can) chickpeas or garbanzo beans, drained
- ⅔ cup (6-ounce can) CONTADINA Italian-Style Tomato Paste
- 8 ounces medium shrimp, cooked
- ½ teaspoon salt
- ¼ teaspoon ground black pepper
- 2 tablespoons chopped fresh Italian parsley or 2 teaspoons dried parsley flakes

In large saucepan, heat oil over medium-high heat. Add onion and garlic; sauté for 1 minute. Stir in broth, tomatoes and juice, chickpeas and tomato paste. Bring to a boil. Reduce heat to low; simmer, uncovered, for 10 minutes. Add shrimp, salt and pepper; simmer for 3 minutes or until heated through. Sprinkle with parsley just before serving.

Artichoke and Olive Salad

Makes 10 servings

- 1 pound dry rotini pasta, cooked, drained, chilled
- 3½ cups (*two* 14.5-ounce cans) CONTADINA Pasta Ready Chunky Tomatoes Primavera, undrained
- ½ cup (6-ounce jar) artichoke hearts, packed in water, drained, sliced
- ½ cup Italian dressing
- ½ cup (2.25-ounce can) sliced pitted ripe olives, drained
- ¼ cup chopped fresh parsley or 2 teaspoons dried parsley flakes, crushed
- ¼ cup sliced green onions
- ½ cup sliced almonds, toasted

In large bowl, combine pasta, tomatoes and juice, artichoke hearts, dressing, olives, parsley and green onions; toss well. Cover. Chill before serving. Sprinkle with almonds just before serving.

Chickpea and Shrimp Soup

PASTA SAUCES

Make any night pasta night! Top off your favorite hot cooked pasta with this enticing collection of select sauces. From traditional Spaghetti Sauce to savory Bolognese Sauce, you're sure to find that perfect sauce to suit your every need.

Giardiniera Sauce

Makes 8 servings

1 tablespoon olive or vegetable oil

2 cups sliced fresh mushrooms

1 cup chopped onion

½ cup sliced green bell pepper

2 cloves garlic, minced

1¾ cups (14.5-ounce can) CONTADINA Stewed Tomatoes, undrained

½ cup chicken broth

⅓ cup (*half* 6-ounce can) CONTADINA Tomato Paste

2 teaspoons Italian herb seasoning

½ teaspoon salt (optional)

1 pound dry pasta, cooked, drained, kept warm

In large skillet, heat oil. Add mushrooms, onion, bell pepper and garlic; sauté for 3 to 4 minutes or until vegetables are tender. Stir in tomatoes and juice, broth, tomato paste, Italian seasoning and salt. Bring to a boil. Reduce heat to low; simmer, uncovered, for 10 minutes, stirring occasionally. Serve over pasta.

Giardiniera Sauce

42

Roma Artichoke and Tomato Ragu

Makes 4 servings

1¾ cups (14.5-ounce can) CONTADINA Recipe Ready Diced Tomatoes, drained
½ cup (6-ounce jar) marinated artichoke hearts, sliced, undrained
¼ cup sliced pitted ripe olives, drained
2 tablespoons chopped fresh parsley or 2 teaspoons dried parsley flakes
2 tablespoons chopped fresh basil or 2 teaspoons dried basil leaves, crushed
1 clove garlic, minced
¼ teaspoon salt
⅛ teaspoon ground black pepper
8 ounces dry pasta, cooked, drained, kept warm
1 tablespoon chopped parsley (optional)

In medium bowl, combine tomatoes, artichoke hearts and juice, olives, parsley, basil, garlic, salt and pepper. Cover; chill for several hours to blend flavors. Heat before serving. Serve over pasta. Sprinkle with parsley, if desired.

Bolognese Sauce

Makes 8 servings

1 tablespoon olive or vegetable oil
1 cup chopped onion
½ cup diced celery
3 cloves garlic, minced
8 ounces lean ground beef
1¾ cups (15-ounce can) CONTADINA Tomato Puree
⅔ cup (6-ounce can) CONTADINA Italian-Style Tomato Paste
½ cup beef broth
⅓ cup dry red wine or water
2 teaspoons chopped fresh marjoram or 1 teaspoon dried marjoram leaves, crushed
1 teaspoon salt (optional)
1 pound dry pasta, cooked, drained, kept warm

In large skillet, heat oil. Add onion, celery and garlic; sauté for 3 to 4 minutes or until vegetables are tender. Add ground beef; cook for 5 to 7 minutes or until evenly browned, stirring occasionally. Add tomato puree, tomato paste, broth, wine, marjoram and salt. Bring to a boil. Reduce heat to low; simmer, uncovered, for 10 to 15 minutes or until heated through, stirring occasionally. Serve over pasta.

Roma Artichoke and Tomato Ragu

Spaghetti Sauce

Makes 8 servings

1 pound mild Italian sausage, casings removed
1 cup chopped onion
1 clove garlic, minced
½ cup sliced fresh mushrooms
3½ cups (28-ounce can) CONTADINA Crushed Tomatoes
2 cups (15-ounce can) CONTADINA Tomato Sauce
½ teaspoon dried oregano leaves, crushed
¼ teaspoon dried basil leaves, crushed
1 pound dry pasta, cooked, drained, kept warm

In large skillet, brown sausage with onion and garlic, stirring to break up sausage. Stir in mushrooms, crushed tomatoes, tomato sauce, oregano and basil. Bring to a boil. Reduce heat to low; simmer, uncovered, for 30 minutes, stirring occasionally. Serve over pasta.

First-Class Pasta Sauce

Makes 8 servings

1 pound lean ground beef
1 cup chopped onion
2 large cloves garlic, minced
3½ cups (*two* 14.5-ounce cans) CONTADINA Recipe Ready Diced Tomatoes, undrained
1⅓ cups (12-ounce can) CONTADINA Tomato Paste
1 cup water
1 cup sliced fresh mushrooms
1 bay leaf
1 to 2 teaspoons dried oregano leaves, crushed
½ to 1 teaspoon dried basil leaves, crushed
1 teaspoon salt
⅛ teaspoon ground black pepper
1 pound dry pasta, cooked, drained, kept warm
½ cup (2 ounces) grated Parmesan cheese

In large skillet, brown ground beef with onion and garlic. Add tomatoes and juice, tomato paste, water, mushrooms, bay leaf, oregano, basil, salt and pepper. Bring to a boil. Reduce heat to low; simmer, uncovered, for 30 minutes, stirring occasionally. Remove bay leaf; discard. Serve sauce over pasta; sprinkle with Parmesan cheese.

Spaghetti Sauce

Italian-Style Tomato Sauce

Makes 8 servings

- ¼ cup butter or margarine
- ½ cup finely chopped onion
- ½ cup shredded peeled carrot
- ½ cup sliced celery
- 3½ cups (28-ounce can) CONTADINA Crushed Tomatoes
- ¼ teaspoon crushed red pepper flakes
- ¼ teaspoon granulated sugar
- ¼ cup heavy whipping cream (optional)
- ¼ cup chopped fresh cilantro
- 1 pound dry pasta, cooked, drained, kept warm

In medium skillet, melt butter. Add onion, carrot and celery; sauté for 3 to 5 minutes or until vegetables are tender. Add crushed tomatoes, red pepper flakes and sugar. Reduce heat to low; simmer, uncovered, for 40 minutes, stirring occasionally. Add cream and cilantro; simmer for 1 minute. Serve over pasta.

Puttenesca Sauce

Makes 8 servings

- 2 tablespoons olive or vegetable oil
- 2 cloves garlic, minced
- 1¾ cups (14.5-ounce can) CONTADINA Recipe Ready Diced Tomatoes, undrained
- 1¼ cups (6-ounce can) sliced pitted ripe olives, drained
- ⅔ cup (6-ounce can) CONTADINA Tomato Paste
- ⅓ cup chopped fresh parsley or 1 tablespoon dried parsley flakes
- ⅓ cup water
- 2 tablespoons dry red wine or chicken broth
- 1 tablespoon capers
- 1 tablespoon Worcestershire sauce
- 1 teaspoon dried oregano leaves, crushed
- ⅛ teaspoon crushed red pepper flakes
- 1 pound dry pasta, cooked, drained, kept warm

In medium skillet, heat oil. Add garlic; sauté for 30 seconds. Stir in tomatoes and juice, olives, tomato paste, parsley, water, wine, capers, Worcestershire sauce, oregano and red pepper flakes. Bring to a boil. Reduce heat to low; simmer, uncovered, for 10 minutes, stirring occasionally. Serve over pasta.

Italian-Style Tomato Sauce

Portofino Primavera

Makes 8 servings

2 tablespoons olive or vegetable
   oil
1 small onion, chopped (about
   1 cup)
1 large clove garlic, minced
1¾ cups (14.5-ounce can)
   CONTADINA Recipe Ready
   Diced Tomatoes, undrained
⅔ cup (6-ounce can)
   CONTADINA Tomato Paste
1 cup chicken broth or water
1 cup quartered sliced zucchini
½ cup sliced pitted ripe olives,
   drained
2 tablespoons capers
½ teaspoon salt
1 pound dry pasta, cooked,
   drained, kept warm

In medium saucepan, heat oil. Add onion and garlic; sauté for 1 minute. Add tomatoes and juice, tomato paste, broth, zucchini, olives, capers and salt. Bring to a boil. Reduce heat to low; simmer, uncovered, for 15 to 20 minutes or until heated through, stirring occasionally. Serve over pasta.

Olive Lovers' Pasta Sauce

Makes 6 servings

1 tablespoon olive or vegetable
   oil
2 cloves garlic, minced
1¾ cups (15-ounce can)
   CONTADINA Tomato Puree
1¾ cups (14.5-ounce can)
   CONTADINA Recipe Ready
   Diced Tomatoes, undrained
½ cup beef broth
1 cup pitted ripe olives, drained,
   quartered
1 cup pitted green olives,
   drained, quartered
¾ cup sliced green onions
¼ cup pine nuts, coarsely
   chopped
1 tablespoon dried basil leaves,
   crushed
½ teaspoon granulated sugar
¼ teaspoon ground black pepper
¾ pound dry pasta, cooked,
   drained, kept warm

In medium skillet, heat oil. Add garlic; sauté for 30 seconds. Stir in tomato puree, tomatoes and juice, broth, olives, green onions, pine nuts, basil, sugar and pepper. Bring to a boil. Reduce heat to low; simmer, uncovered, for 10 to 12 minutes or until heated through, stirring occasionally. Serve over pasta.

Portofino Primavera

Pepperonata

Makes 4 servings

- 3 tablespoons olive or vegetable oil
- 1 *each:* red, yellow and green bell peppers, thinly sliced
- 3 cups thinly sliced red or yellow onion
- 2 large cloves garlic, minced
- 3½ cups (*two* 14.5-ounce cans) CONTADINA Recipe Ready Diced Tomatoes, drained
- 2 tablespoons chopped fresh parsley or 2 teaspoons dried parsley flakes
- 1 tablespoon *plus* 1½ teaspoons balsamic or red wine vinegar
- 1 teaspoon salt
- ½ teaspoon dried thyme leaves, crushed
- ¼ teaspoon ground black pepper
- 8 ounces dry pasta, cooked, drained, kept warm
- 1 tablespoon chopped parsley (optional)

In large skillet, heat oil. Add bell peppers, onion and garlic; sauté for 6 to 8 minutes or until vegetables are tender. Stir in tomatoes, parsley, vinegar, salt, thyme and black pepper; simmer, uncovered, for 12 to 15 minutes or until heated through, stirring occasionally. Serve over pasta. Sprinkle with parsley, if desired.

Tomato-Caper Sauce

Makes 8 servings

- 2 tablespoons olive or vegetable oil
- 2 cloves garlic, minced
- 3½ cups (29-ounce can) CONTADINA Tomato Sauce
- ½ cup capers
- ¼ cup chopped fresh cilantro
- 1 tablespoon chopped fresh basil or 1 teaspoon dried basil leaves, crushed
- 1 tablespoon chopped fresh thyme or 1 teaspoon dried thyme leaves, crushed
- 1 pound dry pasta, cooked, drained, kept warm

In medium saucepan, heat oil. Add garlic; sauté for 30 seconds. Stir in tomato sauce and capers. Bring to a boil. Reduce heat to low; simmer, uncovered, for 20 minutes, stirring occasionally. Stir in cilantro, basil and thyme; simmer for 5 minutes. Serve over pasta.

Pepperonata

MAIN DISHES

Mention Italian entrées and thoughts turn to thick, rich lasagne casseroles and dinner plates piled high with steaming spaghetti covered with delicious sauces. In addition to these recipe classics, this chapter is full of countless other main-dish favorites, such as Baked Rigatoni and Hearty Manicotti.

Hearty Manicotti

Makes 4 to 5 servings

1 package (10 ounces) frozen chopped spinach, thawed, squeezed dry

2 cups (15-ounce container) ricotta cheese

1 egg, lightly beaten

½ cup (2 ounces) grated Parmesan cheese

⅛ teaspoon ground black pepper

8 to 10 dry manicotti shells, cooked, drained

1⅓ cups (*two* 6-ounce cans) CONTADINA Italian-Style Tomato Paste

1⅓ cups water

½ cup (2 ounces) shredded mozzarella cheese

In medium bowl, combine spinach, ricotta cheese, egg, Parmesan cheese and pepper; mix well. Spoon into manicotti shells. Place in ungreased 12×7½-inch baking dish. In small bowl, combine tomato paste and water; pour over manicotti. Sprinkle with mozzarella cheese. Bake in preheated 350°F. oven for 30 to 40 minutes or until heated through.

Hearty Manicotti

Penne with Creamy Tomato Sauce

Makes 4 servings

- 1 tablespoon olive or vegetable oil
- ½ cup diced onion
- 2 tablespoons dry vermouth, white wine or chicken broth
- 1¾ cups (14.5-ounce can) CONTADINA Pasta Ready Chunky Tomatoes Primavera, undrained
- ½ cup heavy whipping cream
- 8 ounces dry penne or rigatoni, cooked, drained, kept warm
- 1 cup pitted ripe olives, drained, sliced
- ½ cup (2 ounces) grated Parmesan cheese
- ¼ cup sliced green onions

In large skillet, heat oil. Add diced onion; sauté for 2 to 3 minutes or until onion is tender. Add vermouth; cook for 1 minute. Stir in tomatoes and juice, cream, pasta, olives and Parmesan cheese; heat thoroughly, stirring occasionally. Sprinkle with green onions.

Eggplant Italiano Open-Faced Sandwiches

Makes 8 servings

- 1 medium eggplant (about 1½ pounds), peeled, cut into 8 slices
- 2 eggs, lightly beaten
- 1 cup CONTADINA Seasoned Bread Crumbs
- ½ cup olive or vegetable oil, *divided*
- 4 sandwich-size English muffins, split, toasted
- 1¾ cups (14.5-ounce can) CONTADINA Pasta Ready Chunky Tomatoes with Olives, drained
- ½ cup (2 ounces) shredded mozzarella cheese

In shallow dish, dip eggplant slices into eggs; coat with bread crumbs. In large skillet, heat *2 tablespoons* oil over medium heat. Add eggplant slices, a few at a time, to skillet. Cook for 2 to 3 minutes on each side or until golden brown. Remove from oil with slotted spoon. Drain on paper towels. Repeat with *remaining* oil and eggplant. Place muffin halves on large, ungreased baking sheet; top with eggplant, tomatoes and cheese. Bake in preheated 350°F. oven for 5 to 7 minutes or until cheese is melted.

Penne with Creamy Tomato Sauce

Lasagne Roll-Ups

Makes 8 servings

1 **pound mild Italian sausage, casings removed**
½ **cup chopped onion**
1 **clove garlic, minced**
1⅓ **cups (12-ounce can) CONTADINA Tomato Paste**
1⅔ **cups water**
1 **teaspoon dried oregano leaves, crushed**
½ **teaspoon dried basil leaves, crushed**
1 **egg**
1 **package (10 ounces) frozen chopped spinach, thawed, squeezed dry**
2 **cups (15-ounce container) ricotta cheese**
1½ **cups (6 ounces) shredded mozzarella cheese, *divided***
1 **cup (4 ounces) grated Parmesan cheese**
½ **teaspoon salt**
¼ **teaspoon ground black pepper**
8 **dry lasagne noodles, cooked, drained, kept warm**

In large skillet, crumble sausage. Add onion and garlic; cook until sausage is no longer pink. Drain. Stir in tomato paste, water, oregano and basil; cover. Bring to a boil. Reduce heat to low; simmer, uncovered, for 20 minutes. In medium bowl, beat egg lightly. Add spinach, ricotta cheese, *1 cup* mozzarella cheese, Parmesan cheese, salt and pepper. Spread about ½ *cup* cheese mixture onto each noodle; roll up. Place,

seam side down, in 12×7½-inch baking dish. Pour sauce over rolls; top with *remaining* mozzarella cheese. Bake in preheated 350°F. oven for 30 to 40 minutes or until heated through.

Vegetables Italiano

Makes 4 servings

2 **tablespoons olive or vegetable oil**
1 **cup sliced peeled carrots**
¾ **cup halved onion slices**
2 **cloves garlic, minced**
1¾ **cups (14.5-ounce can) CONTADINA Stewed Tomatoes, undrained**
3 **cups sliced zucchini**
1 **cup fresh mushrooms, halved**
¼ **teaspoon salt, or to taste**
⅛ **teaspoon ground black pepper**
8 **ounces dry spaghetti, cooked, drained, kept warm**

In large skillet, heat oil. Add carrots, onion and garlic; sauté for 3 minutes. Stir in tomatoes and juice, zucchini, mushrooms, salt and pepper. Bring to a boil. Reduce heat to low; simmer, uncovered, for 5 to 6 minutes or until vegetables are crisp-tender. Serve over spaghetti.

Lasagne Roll-Up

Baked Rigatoni

Makes 8 servings

4 ounces mild Italian sausage, casings removed, sliced
1 cup chopped onion
2 cloves garlic, minced
1¾ cups (14.5-ounce can) CONTADINA Recipe Ready Diced Tomatoes, undrained
⅔ cup (6-ounce can) CONTADINA Tomato Paste
1 cup chicken broth
1 teaspoon salt
1 pound dry rigatoni, cooked, drained, kept warm
1 cup (4 ounces) shredded mozzarella cheese, *divided*
½ cup (2 ounces) shredded Parmesan cheese (optional)
2 tablespoons chopped fresh basil or 2 teaspoons dried basil leaves, crushed

In large skillet, cook sausage for 4 to 6 minutes or until no longer pink. Remove sausage from skillet, reserving any drippings in skillet. Add onion and garlic to skillet; sauté for 2 minutes. Stir in tomatoes and juice, tomato paste, broth and salt. Bring to a boil. Reduce heat to low; simmer, uncovered, for 10 minutes, stirring occasionally. In large bowl, combine pasta, tomato mixture, sausage, *½ cup* mozzarella cheese, Parmesan cheese and basil; spoon into ungreased 13×9-inch baking dish. Sprinkle with *remaining* mozzarella cheese. Bake in preheated 375°F. oven for 10 to 15 minutes or until cheese is melted.

Penne with Shrimp and Vegetables

Makes 6 servings

2 tablespoons olive or vegetable oil
2 medium zucchini, cut into 2-inch strips (about 2 cups)
1 tablespoon minced shallots
8 ounces medium shrimp, peeled, deveined
1 medium yellow bell pepper, cut into strips (about 1 cup)
1¾ cups (14.5-ounce can) CONTADINA Pasta Ready Chunky Tomatoes with Olive Oil, Garlic and Spices, undrained
1 cup sliced pitted ripe olives, drained
1 tablespoon capers
8 ounces dry penne pasta, cooked, drained, kept warm

In large skillet, heat oil. Add zucchini and shallots; sauté for 1 to 2 minutes or until zucchini are crisp-tender. Add shrimp and bell pepper; sauté for 2 to 4 minutes or until shrimp turn pink. Stir in tomatoes and juice, olives and capers; simmer, uncovered, for 2 minutes. Serve with pasta.

Penne with Shrimp and Vegetables

Contadina Classic Lasagne

Makes 10 servings

- 1 **tablespoon olive or vegetable oil**
- 1 **cup chopped onion**
- ½ **cup chopped green bell pepper**
- 2 **cloves garlic, minced**
- 1½ **pounds lean ground beef**
- 3½ **cups (*two* 14.5-ounce cans) CONTADINA Recipe Ready Diced Tomatoes, undrained**
- 1 **cup (8-ounce can) CONTADINA Tomato Sauce**
- ⅔ **cup (6-ounce can) CONTADINA Tomato Paste**
- ½ **cup dry red wine or beef broth**
- 1½ **teaspoons salt**
- 1 **teaspoon dried oregano leaves, crushed**
- 1 **teaspoon dried basil leaves, crushed**
- ½ **teaspoon ground black pepper**
- 1 **egg**
- 1 **cup (8 ounces) ricotta cheese**
- 2 **cups (8 ounces) shredded mozzarella cheese, *divided***
- 1 **pound dry lasagne noodles, cooked, drained, kept warm**

In large skillet, heat oil. Add onion, bell pepper and garlic; sauté for 3 minutes or until vegetables are tender. Add ground beef; cook for 5 to 6 minutes or until evenly browned. Add tomatoes and juice, tomato sauce, tomato paste, wine, salt, oregano, basil and black pepper; bring to a boil. Reduce heat to low; simmer, uncovered, for 20 minutes, stirring occasionally. In medium bowl, beat egg slightly. Stir in ricotta cheese and *1 cup* mozzarella cheese. In ungreased 13×9-inch baking dish, layer noodles, *half* of meat sauce, noodles, all of ricotta cheese mixture, noodles and *remaining* meat sauce. Sprinkle with *remaining* mozzarella cheese. Bake in preheated 350°F. oven for 25 to 30 minutes or until heated through. Let stand for 15 minutes before cutting to serve.

Contadina Classic Lasagne

Italian Garden Fusilli

Makes 6 to 8 servings

1¾ cups (14.5-ounce can)
   CONTADINA Recipe Ready
   Diced Tomatoes, undrained
1 cup (4 ounces) cut fresh green
   beans
¼ teaspoon dried rosemary leaves,
   crushed
½ teaspoon garlic salt
1 small zucchini, thinly sliced
   (about 1 cup)
1 small yellow squash, thinly
   sliced (about 1 cup)
1 cup (12-ounce jar) marinated
   artichoke hearts, undrained
1 cup frozen peas
½ teaspoon salt, or to taste
¼ teaspoon ground black pepper,
   or to taste
8 ounces dry fusilli, cooked,
   drained, kept warm
¼ cup (1 ounce) shredded
   Parmesan cheese

In large skillet, combine tomatoes
and juice, green beans, rosemary
and garlic salt. Bring to a boil.
Reduce heat to low; cover. Simmer
for 3 minutes. Add zucchini and
yellow squash; cover. Simmer for 3
minutes or until vegetables are
tender. Stir in artichoke hearts and
juice, peas, salt and pepper; heat
through. Add pasta; toss to coat well.
Sprinkle with Parmesan cheese just
before serving.

Pasta Primavera with Italian Sausage

Makes 4 servings

8 ounces mild Italian sausage,
   casings removed, sliced
1 small onion, diced (about
   ½ cup)
1 large clove garlic, minced
1 medium zucchini, sliced (about
   1 cup)
1¾ cups (14.5-ounce can)
   CONTADINA Pasta Ready
   Chunky Tomatoes Primavera,
   undrained
½ cup sliced pitted ripe olives,
   drained
¼ cup dry red wine or beef broth
8 ounces dry pasta, cooked,
   drained, kept warm
   Chopped fresh basil (optional)
   Grated Parmesan cheese
   (optional)

In large skillet, cook sausage until no
longer pink. Remove sausage from
skillet, reserving drippings in skillet.
Add onion and garlic to skillet; sauté
for 1 minute. Add zucchini; sauté for
2 minutes. Reduce heat to medium.
Add tomatoes and juice, olives, wine
and sausage; simmer, uncovered, for
5 to 7 minutes or until heated
through. Serve over pasta. Sprinkle
with basil and Parmesan cheese, if
desired.

Italian Garden Fusilli

Italian Rotini Bake

Makes 8 to 10 servings

1 tablespoon olive or vegetable oil
1½ cups chopped onion
2 small zucchini, quartered, sliced (about 1½ cups)
3 cloves garlic, minced
1 pound ground turkey
3½ cups (*two* 14.5-ounce cans) CONTADINA Recipe Ready Diced Tomatoes, undrained
⅔ cup (6-ounce can) CONTADINA Tomato Paste
1 cup water
1 tablespoon Italian herb seasoning
1 teaspoon salt
1 egg
2 cups (15-ounce container) ricotta cheese
3 cups (12 ounces) shredded mozzarella cheese, *divided*
8 ounces dry rotini pasta, cooked, drained, kept warm, *divided*

In large skillet, heat oil over medium-high heat. Add onion, zucchini and garlic; sauté for 2 to 3 minutes or until vegetables are tender. Add turkey; cook for 4 to 5 minutes or until turkey is no longer pink. Drain. Add tomatoes and juice, tomato paste, water, Italian seasoning and salt. Bring to a boil. Reduce heat to low; simmer, uncovered, for 5 minutes. In small bowl, beat egg lightly. Add ricotta cheese and *1 cup* mozzarella cheese. In ungreased 13×9-inch baking dish, layer *half* of pasta and *half* of tomato mixture. Cover with ricotta cheese mixture and *1 cup* mozzarella cheese. Top with *remaining* pasta, tomato mixture and mozzarella cheese. Bake in preheated 350°F. oven for 15 to 20 minutes or until heated through.

Mediterranean Rice

Makes 4 servings

1 tablespoon olive or vegetable oil
⅓ cup chopped onion
1¾ cups (14.5-ounce can) CONTADINA Stewed Tomatoes, undrained
1 cup uncooked long-grain white rice
⅓ cup water
¼ cup canned diced green chiles, drained
¾ teaspoon seasoned salt
½ teaspoon chili powder

In medium saucepan with cover, heat oil. Add onion; sauté for 2 to 3 minutes or until tender. Stir in tomatoes and juice, rice, water, chiles, seasoned salt and chili powder. Bring to a boil; cover. Reduce heat to low. Cook for 20 minutes or until rice is tender and liquid is absorbed, stirring occasionally throughout cooking time to prevent sticking. Fluff rice before serving.

Rotini and Turkey Mozzarella

Makes 8 servings

- 2 tablespoons olive or vegetable oil
- 1½ cups thinly sliced zucchini
- 1 cup chopped onion
- 2 cloves garlic, minced
- 3½ cups (28-ounce can) CONTADINA Crushed Tomatoes
- 2 cups cubed, cooked turkey, chicken, ham or smoked turkey
- ¾ cup whole kernel corn
- 2 teaspoons Italian herb seasoning
- ½ teaspoon salt
- ¼ teaspoon ground black pepper
- 8 ounces dry rotini, cooked, drained
- 1½ cups (6 ounces) shredded mozzarella cheese
- ⅔ cup (about 3 ounces) grated Parmesan cheese
- 3 tablespoons chopped fresh parsley or 1 teaspoon dried parsley flakes

In large skillet, heat oil. Add zucchini, onion and garlic; sauté for 3 to 5 minutes or until vegetables are tender. Stir in crushed tomatoes, turkey, corn, Italian seasoning, salt and pepper. Bring to a boil. Reduce heat to low; simmer, uncovered, for 5 minutes or until heated through. Remove from heat; stir in pasta. Spoon *half* of pasta mixture into greased 13×9-inch baking dish; top with *half* of mozzarella and Parmesan cheeses. Repeat layers.

Bake in preheated 350°F. oven for 20 to 25 minutes or until heated through. Let stand for 5 minutes. Sprinkle with parsley just before serving.

Easy Cheese & Tomato Macaroni

Makes 6 to 8 servings

- 2 packages (7 ounces *each*) macaroni and cheese dinner
- 1 tablespoon olive or vegetable oil
- 1 cup finely chopped onion
- 1 cup thinly sliced celery
- 3½ cups (28-ounce can) CONTADINA Crushed Tomatoes
- Grated Parmesan cheese (optional)
- Sliced green onion or celery leaves (optional)

Cook macaroni (from macaroni and cheese dinner) according to package directions; drain. In large skillet, heat oil. Add chopped onion and celery; sauté for 3 minutes or until vegetables are tender. In small bowl, combine tomatoes and cheese mix from dinner. Stir into vegetable mixture. Simmer for 3 to 4 minutes or until mixture is thickened and heated through. Add macaroni to skillet; stir until well coated with sauce. Heat thoroughly, stirring occasionally. Sprinkle with Parmesan cheese and sliced green onion, if desired.

FISH & POULTRY

Discover how to accent the delicate flavors of fresh fish and tender poultry with this captivating collection of great-tasting Italian-style recipes. Choose from Chicken Marengo, full of chunky fresh vegetables, spicy Shrimp Scampi or a variety of other mouthwatering delicacies.

Poached Seafood Italiano

Makes 4 servings

- **1 tablespoon olive or vegetable oil**
- **1 large clove garlic, minced**
- **¼ cup dry white wine or chicken broth**
- **4 salmon steaks or fillets (6 ounces *each*)**
- **1¾ cups (14.5-ounce can) CONTADINA Pasta Ready Chunky Tomatoes with Olives or Pasta Ready Chunky Tomatoes with Three Cheeses or Pasta Ready Chunky Tomatoes Primavera, undrained**
- **2 tablespoons chopped fresh basil (optional)**

In large skillet, heat oil. Add garlic; sauté for 30 seconds. Add wine. Bring to a boil. Add salmon; cover. Reduce heat to medium; simmer for 6 minutes. Add tomatoes and juice; simmer for 2 minutes or until salmon flakes easily when tested with fork. Sprinkle with basil just before serving, if desired.

Poached Seafood Italiano

Chicken Marengo

Makes 6 servings

2 tablespoons olive or vegetable
   oil
2½ to 3 pounds skinned frying
   chicken pieces or 1½ pounds
   (about 6) boneless, skinless
   chicken breast halves
½ cup chopped onion
½ cup chopped green bell pepper
½ cup sliced fresh mushrooms
1 clove garlic, minced
1¾ cups (14.5-ounce can)
   CONTADINA Recipe Ready
   Diced Tomatoes, undrained
⅔ cup (6-ounce can)
   CONTADINA Tomato Paste
½ cup dry red wine
½ cup chicken broth
1 teaspoon Italian herb seasoning
½ teaspoon salt
⅛ teaspoon ground black pepper

In large skillet, heat oil. Add chicken;
cook until browned on all sides.
Remove chicken from skillet,
reserving any drippings in skillet.
Add onion, bell pepper, mushrooms
and garlic to skillet; sauté for 5
minutes. Add tomatoes and juice,
tomato paste, wine, broth, Italian
seasoning, salt and black pepper.
Return chicken to skillet. Bring to a
boil. Reduce heat to low; cover.
Cook for 30 to 40 minutes or until
chicken is no longer pink in center.
Serve over hot cooked rice or pasta,
if desired.

Note: Red wine can be omitted.
Increase chicken broth to 1 cup.

Seafarers' Supper

Makes 4 to 6 servings

1 tablespoon olive or vegetable
   oil
1 cup chopped green bell pepper
½ cup chopped onion
2 cloves garlic, minced
1¾ cups (14.5-ounce can)
   CONTADINA Italian-Style
   Stewed Tomatoes, undrained
1 cup chicken broth
⅔ cup (6-ounce can)
   CONTADINA Italian-Style
   Tomato Paste
¼ teaspoon salt
¼ teaspoon ground black pepper
1 pound orange roughy, cut into
   1-inch pieces
12 ounces dry linguine, cooked,
   drained, kept warm
   Chopped fresh Italian parsley
   (optional)

In large skillet, heat oil. Add bell
pepper, onion and garlic; sauté for 3
minutes or until vegetables are crisp-
tender. Stir in tomatoes and juice,
broth, tomato paste, salt and black
pepper. Bring to a boil. Reduce heat
to low; simmer, uncovered, for 5
minutes. Add orange roughy; simmer
for 5 minutes or until fish flakes
easily when tested with fork. Spoon
over pasta. Sprinkle with parsley, if
desired.

Chicken Marengo

Shrimp Scampi

Makes 4 servings

- **2 tablespoons olive or vegetable oil**
- **½ cup diced onion**
- **1 large clove garlic, minced**
- **1 small green bell pepper, cut into strips**
- **1 small yellow bell pepper, cut into strips**
- **8 ounces medium shrimp, peeled, deveined**
- **1¾ cups (14.5-ounce can) CONTADINA Pasta Ready Chunky Tomatoes with Crushed Red Pepper, undrained**
- **2 tablespoons chopped fresh parsley or 2 teaspoons dried parsley flakes**
- **1 tablespoon lime juice**
- **½ teaspoon salt**

In large skillet, heat oil over medium-high heat. Add onion and garlic; sauté for 1 minute. Add bell peppers; sauté for 2 minutes. Add shrimp; cook for 2 minutes or until shrimp turn pink. Add tomatoes and juice, parsley, lime juice and salt; cook for 2 to 3 minutes or until heated through. Serve over hot cooked rice or pasta, if desired.

Tomato Tarragon Chicken

Makes 8 servings

- **⅓ cup all-purpose flour**
- **4 teaspoons garlic powder, *divided***
- **1 teaspoon lemon pepper**
- **2 pounds (about 8) boneless, skinless chicken breast halves**
- **2 tablespoons olive or vegetable oil**
- **3½ cups (28-ounce can) CONTADINA Crushed Tomatoes**
- **2 cups sliced fresh mushrooms**
- **2 teaspoons dried tarragon leaves, crushed**
- **½ teaspoon seasoned salt, or to taste**
- **4 to 6 drops hot pepper sauce**

In large plastic food storage bag, combine flour, *2 teaspoons* garlic powder and lemon pepper. Add chicken pieces, 1 at a time; shake to coat evenly. Set aside. In large skillet, heat oil. Add chicken; cook until browned on both sides. Add tomatoes, mushrooms, *remaining* garlic powder, tarragon, seasoned salt and hot pepper sauce; stir to blend. Cover; cook for 10 to 15 minutes or until chicken is no longer pink in center.

Shrimp Scampi

Turkey Roulade

Makes 10 servings

1½ **pounds (10 slices) uncooked, boneless turkey breast**
2 **cups (15-ounce container) ricotta cheese**
1½ **cups (6 ounces) shredded mozzarella cheese, *divided***
1 **package (10 ounces) frozen chopped spinach, thawed, squeezed dry**
½ **teaspoon garlic salt**
1 **tablespoon olive or vegetable oil**
½ **cup chopped onion**
2 **cloves garlic, minced**
1¾ **cups (14.5-ounce can) CONTADINA Recipe Ready Diced Tomatoes, undrained**
⅔ **cup (6-ounce can) CONTADINA Tomato Paste**
1 **cup chicken broth**
1 **teaspoon Italian herb seasoning**
1 **teaspoon salt**
¼ **teaspoon ground black pepper**

Pound turkey slices between 2 pieces of plastic wrap to ⅛-inch thickness. In medium bowl, combine ricotta cheese, *1 cup* mozzarella cheese, spinach and garlic salt. Spread *⅓ cup* cheese mixture onto each turkey slice; roll up. Secure with toothpicks. Place rolls in greased 13×9-inch baking dish. In large skillet, heat oil. Add onion and garlic; sauté for 2 minutes. Add tomatoes and juice, tomato paste, broth, Italian seasoning, salt and pepper. Bring to a boil. Reduce heat to low; simmer, uncovered, for 10 minutes. Spoon sauce over rolls;

cover. Bake in preheated 425°F. oven for 20 to 25 minutes or until turkey is done. Sprinkle with *remaining* mozzarella cheese. Bake for 5 minutes or until cheese is melted.

Clams Diablo

Makes 6 servings

2 **tablespoons olive or vegetable oil**
½ **cup chopped onion**
1 **clove garlic, minced**
1¾ **cups (14.5-ounce can) CONTADINA Recipe Ready Diced Tomatoes, undrained**
¼ **cup dry red wine or chicken broth**
½ **teaspoon dried thyme leaves, crushed**
¼ **teaspoon salt**
¼ **teaspoon crushed red pepper flakes**
1½ **pounds scrubbed fresh clams**
2 **tablespoons chopped fresh parsley or 2 teaspoons dried parsley flakes**

In medium skillet, heat oil. Add onion and garlic; sauté for 1 minute. Stir in tomatoes and juice, wine, thyme, salt and red pepper flakes. Bring to a boil. Reduce heat to low; simmer, uncovered, for 10 minutes, stirring occasionally. Add clams; cover. Simmer for 5 minutes or until clams have opened. Discard any clams that do not open. Sprinkle with parsley just before serving.

Turkey Roulade

Seafood Marinara with Linguine

Makes 6 servings

- **2 tablespoons olive or vegetable oil,** *divided*
- **1 cup chopped onion**
- **3 large cloves garlic, minced**
- **1¾ cups (14.5-ounce can) CONTADINA Recipe Ready Diced Tomatoes, undrained**
- **1¾ cups (14.5-ounce can) chicken broth**
- **1⅓ cups (12-ounce can) CONTADINA Tomato Paste**
- **½ cup dry red wine or water**
- **1 tablespoon chopped fresh basil or 2 teaspoons dried basil leaves, crushed**
- **2 teaspoons chopped fresh oregano or ½ teaspoon dried oregano leaves, crushed**
- **1 teaspoon salt**
- **8 ounces fresh or frozen medium shrimp, peeled, deveined**
- **8 ounces fresh or frozen bay scallops**
- **1 pound dry linguine, cooked, drained, kept warm**

In large skillet, heat *1 tablespoon* oil. Add onion and garlic; sauté for 2 minutes. Add tomatoes and juice, broth, tomato paste, wine, basil, oregano and salt. Bring to a boil. Reduce heat to low; simmer, uncovered, for 10 minutes. In small skillet, heat *remaining* oil. Add shrimp and scallops; sauté for 3 to 4 minutes or until shrimp turn pink. Add to sauce; simmer for 2 to 3 minutes or until heated through. Serve over pasta.

Chicken Italiano

Makes 6 to 8 servings

- **1½ to 2 pounds (6 to 8) boneless, skinless chicken breast halves**
- **¼ cup all-purpose flour**
- **3 tablespoons olive or vegetable oil,** *divided*
- **2 cups sliced onion**
- **⅔ cup (6-ounce can) CONTADINA Tomato Paste**
- **1¾ cups (14.5-ounce can) chicken broth**
- **3 medium carrots, peeled, sliced (about 1½ cups)**
- **2 teaspoons garlic salt**
- **1 teaspoon Italian herb seasoning**
- **⅛ teaspoon crushed red pepper flakes (optional)**
- **2 medium zucchini, sliced (about 1½ cups)**

In shallow bowl, coat chicken with flour. In large skillet, heat *2 tablespoons* oil over medium-high heat. Add chicken; cook for 2 to 3 minutes on each side or until golden brown. Remove chicken from skillet. Add *remaining* oil to skillet; heat. Add onion; sauté until tender. Stir in tomato paste, broth, carrots, garlic salt, Italian seasoning and red pepper flakes. Return chicken to skillet; spoon sauce over chicken. Bring to a boil. Reduce heat to low; cover. Simmer for 25 minutes or until chicken is no longer pink in center. Add zucchini; simmer for 5 minutes. Serve over hot cooked pasta, if desired.

Seafood Marinara with Linguine

Chicken and Vegetable Ragoût

Makes 6 servings

- 2 tablespoons olive or vegetable oil
- ½ cup chopped onion
- 3 cloves garlic, minced
- 1 pound (about 4) boneless, skinless chicken breast halves, cut into ½-inch pieces
- 1 cup water or chicken broth
- 1¾ cups (14.5-ounce can) CONTADINA Recipe Ready Diced Tomatoes, undrained
- ⅔ cup (6-ounce can) CONTADINA Italian-Style Tomato Paste
- 1 cup sliced peeled carrots
- 1 cup halved zucchini slices
- 1 cup red or green bell pepper strips
- 1 teaspoon Italian herb seasoning
- ½ teaspoon salt
- ⅛ teaspoon ground black pepper

In large skillet, heat oil. Add onion and garlic; sauté for 2 to 3 minutes or until onion is tender. Add chicken; cook until browned, stirring frequently. Add water, tomatoes and juice, tomato paste and carrots; cover. Bring to a boil. Reduce heat to low; simmer for 10 minutes, stirring occasionally. Add zucchini, bell pepper, Italian seasoning, salt and black pepper; cover. Simmer for 15 to 20 minutes or until chicken is no longer pink in center and vegetables are tender. Serve over hot cooked rice or pasta, if desired.

Sicilian Fish and Rice Bake

Makes 6 servings

- 3 tablespoons olive or vegetable oil
- ¾ cup chopped onion
- ½ cup chopped celery
- 1 clove garlic, minced
- ½ cup uncooked long-grain white rice
- 3½ cups (*two* 14.5-ounce cans) CONTADINA Recipe Ready Diced Tomatoes, undrained
- 1 teaspoon salt
- 1 teaspoon ground black pepper
- ½ teaspoon granulated sugar
- ⅛ teaspoon cayenne pepper
- 1 pound fish fillets (any firm white fish)
- ¼ cup finely chopped fresh parsley

In large skillet, heat oil. Add onion, celery and garlic; sauté for 2 to 3 minutes or until vegetables are tender. Stir in rice; sauté for 5 minutes or until rice browns slightly. Add tomatoes and juice, salt, black pepper, sugar and cayenne pepper; mix well. Place fish in bottom of greased 12×7½-inch baking dish. Spoon rice mixture over fish; cover with foil. Bake in preheated 400°F. oven for 45 to 50 minutes or until rice is tender. Let stand for 5 minutes before serving. Sprinkle with parsley.

Chicken and Vegetable Ragoût

Swordfish Messina Style

Makes 8 servings

2 tablespoons olive or vegetable oil
½ cup chopped fresh parsley
2 tablespoons chopped fresh basil or 2 teaspoons dried basil leaves, crushed
2 cloves garlic, minced
1 cup (8-ounce can) CONTADINA Tomato Sauce
¾ cup sliced fresh mushrooms
1 tablespoon capers
1 tablespoon lemon juice
⅛ teaspoon ground black pepper
3 pounds swordfish or halibut steaks

In small saucepan, heat oil. Add parsley, basil and garlic; sauté for 1 minute. Reduce heat to low. Add tomato sauce, mushrooms and capers. Bring to a boil. Reduce heat to low; simmer, uncovered, for 5 minutes. Stir in lemon juice and pepper. Place swordfish in single layer in greased 13×9-inch baking dish; cover with sauce. Bake in preheated 400°F. oven for 20 minutes or until fish flakes easily when tested with fork.

Chicken in Cilantro Sauce

Makes 6 servings

1 tablespoon olive or vegetable oil
1 *each:* small green, red and yellow bell peppers, sliced into ¼-inch-thick rings
1½ pounds (about 6) boneless, skinless chicken breast halves
2 cups (15-ounce can) CONTADINA Tomato Sauce
½ cup chopped fresh cilantro
½ cup coarsely chopped onion
1 clove garlic, minced
⅛ teaspoon salt

In medium skillet, heat oil. Add bell peppers; sauté until crisp-tender. Remove peppers from skillet, reserving any liquid in skillet. Add chicken to skillet; cook until browned on both sides. Remove skillet from heat; cover to keep chicken warm. In blender container, place tomato sauce, cilantro, onion, garlic and salt; blend until smooth. Pour over chicken in skillet. Return skillet to heat. Bring to a boil. Reduce heat to low; simmer, uncovered, for 15 to 20 minutes or until chicken is no longer pink in center. Remove chicken to serving platter; top with peppers. Serve with sauce.

Swordfish Messina Style

Skillet Chicken Cacciatore

Makes 6 servings

- **2 tablespoons olive or vegetable oil**
- **1 cup sliced red onion**
- **1 medium green bell pepper, cut into strips (about 1 cup)**
- **2 cloves garlic, minced**
- **1 pound (about 4) boneless, skinless chicken breast halves**
- **1¾ cups (14.5-ounce can) CONTADINA Pasta Ready Chunky Tomatoes with Mushrooms, undrained**
- **¼ cup dry white wine or chicken broth**
- **½ teaspoon salt**
- **¼ teaspoon ground black pepper**
- **1 tablespoon chopped fresh basil or 1 teaspoon dried basil leaves, crushed**

In large skillet, heat oil over medium-high heat. Add onion, bell pepper and garlic; sauté for 1 minute. Add chicken; cook until browned on both sides. Add tomatoes and juice, wine, salt and black pepper. Bring to a boil. Reduce heat to low; simmer, uncovered, for 15 to 20 minutes or until chicken is no longer pink in center. Serve over hot cooked rice or pasta, if desired. Sprinkle with basil.

Tomato and Salmon Quiche

Makes 6 servings

- **1 tablespoon olive or vegetable oil**
- **1½ cups chopped fresh mushrooms**
- **½ cup chopped shallots**
- **1¾ cups (14.5-ounce can) CONTADINA Recipe Ready Diced Tomatoes, drained**
- **½ teaspoon salt**
- **¼ teaspoon ground white pepper**
- **1¾ cups (*two* 7½-ounce cans) LIBBY'S Pacific Keta or Pink Salmon, drained**
- **3 tablespoons thinly sliced green onion**
- **2 tablespoons grated Parmesan cheese**
- **3 eggs**
- **¾ cup heavy whipping cream**
- **1 *unbaked* 9-inch pie shell**

In medium skillet, heat oil. Add mushrooms and shallots; sauté for 2 minutes. Stir in tomatoes, salt and pepper. Cook for 2 minutes or until most of liquid is evaporated. Remove from heat. Remove skin and bones from salmon, if desired; discard. Stir salmon, green onion and Parmesan cheese into mushroom mixture. In medium bowl, beat eggs lightly; stir in cream. Bake pie shell in preheated 400°F. oven for 5 minutes. Spoon salmon filling into hot pie shell; pour egg mixture over filling. Bake at 350°F. for 25 minutes or until center is set. Let stand for 5 minutes before cutting to serve.

Skillet Chicken Cacciatore

Italian Chicken Stir-Fry

Makes 4 servings

2 tablespoons olive or vegetable oil
1 pound (about 4) boneless, skinless chicken breast halves, cut into strips
½ cup chopped green bell pepper
½ cup chopped onion
1 large clove garlic, minced
1 cup sliced fresh mushrooms
2 medium zucchini, sliced (about 1 cup)
1¾ cups (14.5-ounce can) CONTADINA Recipe Ready Diced Tomatoes, undrained
2 tablespoons capers
1 tablespoon chopped fresh basil or 1 teaspoon dried basil leaves, crushed
½ teaspoon Italian herb seasoning
¼ teaspoon salt
⅛ teaspoon crushed red pepper flakes
1 tablespoon cornstarch

In large skillet, heat oil. Add chicken, bell pepper, onion and garlic; sauté for 3 to 4 minutes or until chicken is lightly browned. Add mushrooms and zucchini; sauté for 2 to 3 minutes or until zucchini are crisp-tender. Drain tomatoes, reserving juice in small bowl. Add tomatoes, capers, basil, Italian seasoning, salt and red pepper flakes to skillet. Add cornstarch to reserved tomato juice; mix well. Stir into mixture in skillet. Cook, stirring constantly, until liquid is thickened. Serve over hot cooked rice, if desired.

Chicken with Artichokes and Basil

Makes 6 servings

2 tablespoons olive or vegetable oil
2½ to 3 pounds skinned frying chicken pieces or 1½ pounds (about 6) boneless, skinless chicken breast halves
1 cup thinly sliced peeled carrots
1 cup sliced fresh mushrooms
½ cup chopped onion
1 clove garlic, minced
2 cups (15-ounce can) CONTADINA Tomato Sauce
½ cup dry white wine or chicken broth
1 tablespoon chopped fresh basil or 1 teaspoon dried basil leaves, crushed
¾ teaspoon salt
¼ teaspoon ground black pepper
½ cup (4-ounce can) artichoke hearts packed in water, drained

In large skillet, heat oil. Add chicken; cook until browned on both sides. Remove chicken from skillet, reserving drippings in skillet. Add carrots, mushrooms, onion and garlic to skillet; sauté for 2 to 3 minutes or until vegetables are tender. Return chicken to skillet. Add tomato sauce, wine, basil, salt and pepper; cover. Bring to a boil. Reduce heat to low; simmer, uncovered, for 30 minutes. Add artichoke hearts; simmer for 10 minutes or until chicken is no longer pink in center.

Saucy Turkey Rolls

Makes 4 servings

1 **tablespoon olive or vegetable oil**
½ **cup chopped onion**
1 **clove garlic, minced**
2 **cups (15-ounce can) CONTADINA Tomato Sauce**
2 **teaspoons chopped fresh rosemary or ½ teaspoon dried rosemary, crushed**
½ **teaspoon Italian herb seasoning**
½ **teaspoon salt**
⅛ **teaspoon ground black pepper**
1 **pound (4 slices) uncooked, boneless turkey breast**
4 **ounces thinly sliced fontina cheese**
8 **green onions, cut into 4-inch pieces**
2 **tablespoons butter or margarine**
¼ **cup dry white wine or chicken broth**

In large skillet, heat oil. Add onion and garlic; sauté for 1 minute. Stir in tomato sauce, rosemary, Italian seasoning, salt and pepper. Bring to a boil. Reduce heat to low; simmer, uncovered, for 15 minutes. Pound turkey slices between 2 pieces of plastic wrap to ⅛-inch thickness; top each turkey slice with 1 slice cheese and 2 green onion pieces. Roll up turkey; secure with toothpicks. In medium skillet, melt butter. Add turkey rolls; cook until browned on all sides. Pour wine over turkey rolls. Reduce heat to low; cover. Simmer for 10 minutes or until turkey is done. Serve sauce over turkey rolls and hot cooked pasta, if desired.

Note: Substitute 1 pound veal cutlets for turkey breast slices.

MEATS

With a simple, delicious Italian sauce, you can transform beef, sausage or any other meat into an authentic Italian main dish. Try fresh-tasting Italian Sausage Supper or Baked Steak Flamenco tonight.

Italian-Style Meat Loaf

Makes 8 servings

1 egg

1½ pounds lean ground beef or turkey

8 ounces hot or mild Italian sausage, casings removed

1 cup CONTADINA Seasoned Bread Crumbs

1 cup (8-ounce can) CONTADINA Tomato Sauce, *divided*

1 cup finely chopped onion

½ cup finely chopped green bell pepper

In large bowl, beat egg lightly. Add ground beef, sausage, bread crumbs, *¾ cup* tomato sauce, onion and bell pepper; mix well. Press into ungreased 9×5-inch loaf pan. Bake, uncovered, in preheated 350°F. oven for 60 minutes. Spoon *remaining* tomato sauce over meat loaf. Bake for an additional 15 minutes or until no longer pink in center; drain. Let stand for 10 minutes before serving.

Italian-Style Meat Loaf

Sirloin Steak Monte Carlo

Makes 4 to 6 servings

- 2 tablespoons olive or vegetable oil
- 1¾ pounds sirloin steak
- ½ cup sliced onion
- 1 large clove garlic, minced
- ¼ cup pine nuts
- 1¾ cups (14.5-ounce can) CONTADINA Italian-Style Tomatoes, undrained
- 2 tablespoons capers
- ½ teaspoon dried oregano leaves, crushed
- ½ teaspoon dried basil leaves, crushed
- ¼ teaspoon crushed red pepper flakes

In medium skillet, heat oil over medium-high heat. Add steak; cook for 4 to 5 minutes on each side for medium-rare. Remove steak to platter, reserving any drippings in skillet; keep warm. Add onion, garlic and pine nuts to skillet; sauté for 5 minutes or until onion is tender and nuts are lightly toasted. Add tomatoes and juice, capers, oregano, basil and red pepper flakes; simmer, uncovered, for 5 minutes. Serve over steak.

Sloppy Joes

Makes 4 servings

- 8 ounces lean ground beef or turkey
- ½ cup finely chopped onion
- ½ cup CONTADINA Pizza Sauce
- 2 sandwich-size English muffins, split, toasted
- ½ cup (2 ounces) shredded cheddar cheese

In medium skillet, brown ground beef with onion; drain. Stir in pizza sauce; simmer, uncovered, for 5 to 8 minutes or until heated through, stirring occasionally. Spoon mixture evenly onto muffin halves; sprinkle with cheese. Broil 6 to 8 inches from heat for 1 to 2 minutes or until cheese is melted.

Sirloin Steak Monte Carlo

Italian Sausage Supper

Makes 6 servings

1 pound mild Italian sausage, casings removed
1 cup chopped onion
3 medium zucchini, sliced (about 1½ cups)
⅔ cup (6-ounce can) CONTADINA Tomato Paste
1 cup water
1 teaspoon dried basil leaves, crushed
½ teaspoon salt
3 cups cooked rice
1 cup (4 ounces) shredded mozzarella cheese
¼ cup (1 ounce) grated Romano cheese

In large skillet, brown sausage with onion, stirring to break up sausage; drain, reserving 1 tablespoon drippings. Spoon sausage mixture into greased 2-quart casserole dish. Add zucchini to skillet; sauté for 5 minutes or until crisp-tender. In medium bowl, combine tomato paste, water, basil and salt. Stir in rice. Spoon over sausage mixture. Arrange zucchini slices on top; sprinkle with mozzarella and Romano cheeses. Cover. Bake in preheated 350°F. oven for 20 minutes.

Baked Steak Flamenco

Makes 6 servings

¼ cup all-purpose flour
½ teaspoon seasoned salt
⅛ teaspoon ground black pepper
1½ pounds trimmed round steak, cut into strips
½ cup thinly sliced onion
1 cup thin green bell pepper rings
1 cup sliced fresh mushrooms
1¾ cups (14.5-ounce can) CONTADINA Italian-Style Tomatoes, undrained
¼ cup horseradish sauce
1 tablespoon Worcestershire sauce

In large bowl or plastic food storage bag, combine flour, seasoned salt and black pepper. Add steak; toss to coat evenly. Place in greased 13×9-inch baking dish. Arrange onion, bell pepper and mushrooms on top of steak. Drain tomatoes, reserving juice. Slice tomatoes lengthwise; arrange on top of vegetables. In small bowl, combine reserved juice, horseradish sauce and Worcestershire sauce; pour evenly over all ingredients in baking dish. Bake, uncovered, in preheated 350°F. oven for 45 minutes to 1 hour or until steak is desired doneness.

Italian Sausage Supper

Veal Parmesan

Makes 4 servings

½ **cup CONTADINA Seasoned Bread Crumbs**

¼ **cup (1 ounce) grated Parmesan cheese**

1 **pound thin veal cutlets**

1 **egg, lightly beaten**

3 **tablespoons olive or vegetable oil, *divided***

4 **ounces mozzarella cheese, thinly sliced**

¼ **cup finely chopped onion**

1 **clove garlic, minced**

1 **cup (8-ounce can) CONTADINA Tomato Sauce**

1 **tablespoon chopped fresh oregano or 1 teaspoon dried oregano leaves, crushed**

In shallow dish, combine bread crumbs and Parmesan cheese. Dip veal into egg; coat with crumb mixture. In large skillet, heat *2 tablespoons* oil over medium-high heat. Add veal; cook until golden brown on both sides. Drain on paper towels. Place veal on ovenproof platter; top with mozzarella cheese. Bake in preheated 350°F. oven for 5 to 10 minutes or until cheese is melted. Heat *remaining* oil in medium saucepan. Add onion and garlic; sauté for 1 to 2 minutes or until onion is tender. Stir in tomato sauce and oregano. Bring to a boil. Reduce heat to low; simmer, uncovered, for 5 to 10 minutes or until heated through. Serve sauce over veal.